Neolithic Imaginings

Mythic Explorations of the Unknown

Neolithic Imaginings

Mythic Explorations of the Unknown

Poems by

Loralee Clark

Cover design by Shay Culligan
Cover image by Loralee Clark
Author photo by Loralee Clark
First graphic by Round Icons on Unsplash
Last graphic by Public Domain Vectors on Unsplash

ISBN: 979-8-90146-824-1
Library of Congress Control Number: 2026936264

Kelsay Books
502 South 1040 East, A-119
American Fork, Utah 84003
Kelsaybooks.com

Love and Gratitude to my biggest cheerleaders:
Cara Finnegan and Susan Zickle;
without your realism, positive energy,
and friendship, I would never come out to play.

For your help with my poetry and craft-building:
Teresa Burns Murphy, Suzanne Koopmans,
Ann Chinnis, Jennifer Randall Hotz,
Thayer Cory, and Luisa Igloria.

For your humor, creativity, and love:
Christopher Carone, Ian Carone,
and Sal Carone.

Acknowledgments

Thank you to the following publications, in which versions of these poems previously appeared:

Arkansas Scottish Festival, 2024 Celtic Poetry Contest:
“Dolmen/Tinkinswood Burial Chamber: Tinkinswood, Wales” (2nd place)
Cannon’s Mouth: “Loch an Duin Crannog, Scotland”
Dawntreader: “Brynn Celi Ddu: Mound in the Dark Grove”
Everscribe: “Stonehenge: Ecology of Flux”
Heart on Our Sleeves: “Göbekli Tepe”
Lucky Lizard Journal: “Swinside: Holy Engineering”
“Dolman/Tinkinswood Burial Chamber: Tinkinswood, Wales”
Nebo: “Avebury Henge”
The Orchards Poetry Journal: “Woodhenge, Salisbury, England: What Holds a Culture Together”
Roots and Leaves by *Wingless Dreamer:* “Rollright, England: Extended Cognition”
Veritas & Arcana (anthology, Elixir Verse Press): “Sacred Shape”
White Stag Journal’s Blood Lore: “Meini Hirion, Wales: Lunating”

Two poems were first published in a chapbook:

Solemnity Rites (Prolific Pulse Press, 2025): “Brynn Celi Ddu: Mound in the Dark Grove,” “Göbekli Tepe”

Contents

Sacred Shape

A snake eating itself;
no beginning and no end,
water dropping from a cloud
rippling a pond
or sap seeping from a cut
in the bark, filling a bucket
ready to boil to sweetness.

Our eyes' iris and pupil,
our areolas, nipples, breasts;
circles within circles.
Like a ring in our ear or
around our fingers like love
everlasting: infinity creating other life
to carry on our cooking, cleaning, caring
telling the stories of who came before us;
our bodies and the knowledge they contain:
a merry-go-round of generations that
contain another kind of sweetness.

Even larger circles: the sky's stars,
inaccessible through distance, through time
but still sheltering us with their light.
We read their patterns, find meaning, give directions
tell our ancestors' stories to shape cultures.
We walk outside at night and list
the ones we know: big dipper, Orion,
Betelgeuse, Vega.

Larger still is the way movement pours from our planet
spinning through space around a closer star, Helios:
a circle of gas and heat shaping life
on our own molten circle.

Göbekli Tepe

This is the story of the people who studied the endless above,
who opened their hearts to the endless above,
the lineage of Natufians and their progeny,
constructing observatories as an equal-sided triangle:
holy geometry—the first pyramid, flat and strong in its creativity.

This is the story of the people who saw in the stars
the animals, the shapes of purpose,
constellating themselves as pictures of the night,
bright like the moon's body.

This is the story of the people
who shaped their bodies as songs to be sung together, whole,
as the moon grew and shrunk in rhythm,
stood in this place to converse with stars,
mapping the perpetual cycles of sky.

And when the endless above crashed into the earth,
when heaven's stars caused fires and a great flooding,
the waters pulled stones from the mountains,
roots were pulled from the mountains like sheaves of emmer
and soon all was eclipsed. The people too went dark:
their throats stung, the coughing endless.
They spat and shat ash, eyes flowing with tears;
baskets of dried turmeric emptied long before they had finished
    dying.

Had they not heard the endless above's singing?
Had the people not heard the vulture, the scorpion well enough
to understand this impending doom?

Surely the sky had warned of its disaster:
fire, flooding, storms and darkness?
The people had not been prepared as death came
hot and fiery, currented sudden and strong.

Those who could, with their crusted, weeping eyes,
with their burning chests and shortened breath,
dug a womb in the earth to escape,
the lost sky unable to speak of place.

When time slowed again,
when breathing began to deepen in their lungs,
they met and deliberated:
What if their tongues could no longer move breath forward?
What if their breath could no longer measure the stories of the
people?
Who would tell of the stars' visit,
who would recreate the clouds of ash,
to warn that this might happen again?
What if all to stay would be the heavy brown air
in lungs which cannot tell the stories?

Dirt and sand erode over lifetimes, leaving rivulets, pock marks,
but the stone temple did not; the people prayed to the rocks,
the people asked the rocks to share their knowledge,
they prayed to the vulture in the rock, carving its outstretched wing
carving into the pillar as the stars had carved into the mountains,
taking away what had always been there,
to fossilize the people's memories into the rock's language.

The people sought to fix their story in the rock's language
in case they could not carry this history through the air of their
    bodies;
in case they were carried away again from beloved valleys and
    plains.
It was decided and the people let these stones serve as solid
    witness;
stone has seen since the beginning
and would help mark that time of dying and flood.

When the long work was finished, when the slabs were erected
when the praying, carving, dying and recovering had come to pass
some were ready to leave, to look for people
who may not have departed into the great beyond
into the screams and tears, carried away in the rushing waters.
Some left to care for others, to carry stories, guidance, compassion.
Tall and sure, some carried these tools,
arms open like pages ready to be read, to look for stones,
to teach others to dig and mark,
place and carve the noises living on our breath
to pass the knowing into the stones
mirroring the time when the stars themselves kissed the ground,
pushing chaos into becoming.
They practiced polishing their invisible fascia with the stars.

Standing Stones of Stenness, Ring O' Brodgar, Ring O' Bookan

In Orkney, the air thick with humidity,
the sun dying in pinks and oranges,
like midwinter for the past tens of thousands of years
they begin at Stennes: clay vessels of honey
left at the stones. They travel across the moors,
measured sure-footedness, afar from the corries and crags,
their breath preceding them.

They travel straight through to Brodgar,
their wind-chapped fingers sloughing
against its pitted pillars, juniper and
dried rose sprinkled in the small fire there.

On to Bookan, through frosted bracken and heather
to enter this third terrestrial star, its fire burning intensely
in the cup's center of the ring.

They have made their way to see the band of three stars
rising at the west end of the ring, these stars carved in stone
they have just walked past on foot. These mother stars,
three torches, born above each of their heads.

They place rowan branches in this last fire for protection,
pine branches, sap snapping in the heat for eternal life,
bundled and knotted oat straw for nourishment in the coming year.

As they sing, voices and melodies rolling and bobbing like the
ocean's tide,
lungs stinging with cold, they are a mirror to the great above in
each direction:
north, earth; west, winter; south, fire; and east, summer.
They are a cartography of relationships: themselves and the land,
the sun's seasons, the stars' language and the moon's time.

They move about the circle celebrating these calendars of truth.

Dolmen/Tinkinswood Burial Chamber; Tinkinswood, Wales

Next to the chamber lay a long stone, sideways
like an animal's torso: a pit carved
where a shoulder would connect,
sharpening areas like ribs along the flank.

Those engineers began using the wisdom
of earth's bones: stone to cut stone,
sharp blows reverberating, shaking flesh
to shape where they rhapsodized, exalted
the living divine, the soul to be reborn.

These alchemists
pregnant with curiosity,
chests blooming like linden trees,
fragrant and light
assembled three stones, recited the names
of all who came before, beginning in darkness,
relying on their inner sight
navigating plains of desire.

If you fall asleep here, under the rock roof,
it is prophesized you will die, go mad,
or become a poet: decode my fate. I woke
seeing snakes, umbilicus of this earth,
healthy, vital, sweet, cool, rope wriggling,
shedding itself to cast off death:
a new moon with her own rebirth.

Grass snake, moon snake,
brown beauty blessing this stone,
slinking away to multiply herself,
build the mountains: world born from her seed.

Stonehenge: Ecology of Flux

Breath is the air where the ancestors live;
they fill your lungs that you may speak
before you sing:
a stitch in the web of us.

With many ascending to the stars
they lay threads of knowing,
cocoon cumulative around us in this cup and ring,
moving this lymph, embroidering
this tapestry of living to itself—
one syllable decay, the next rebirth.

Settle our spirits
ground us to place

One tribe begins low, multioctave:
we mirror the stones
which mirror stars moving through our bodies,
our bodies moving through the air,
air through our mouths:
we become the stars.

Hear us sing
reverberating these stones

Another tribe begins, another falls along
like a hint, a suggestion:
powerful medicine, a blessing.

We are a tidepool holding the tension and gradient
that comes with the inhale,
before the exhale—
building bones, sheathing flesh:

Settle our spirts
ground us to place
hear the stars sing
through these stones.

Breath is the air where ancestors live,
a stitch in the web of the collective.

Rollright, England: Extended Cognition

We send our questions with the logs of pine, the black henbane.
We send questions into the fire, inhaling smoke plumes
as trees and meadow read the stars' maps embedded in our bones.
We lift and lay the slabs, our ladder to the stars,
healing and fortifying, energy flowing from the plants and smoke
through our chests into the stones, singing itself to sky.

We laid the boulders of this compass rose, this womb, cup of spirit
rings rippling outward, a path leading into the center: balance,
wholeness, writing our presence on the land,
scribing our roots above the ground.

We read the moon's face, hanging,
whispering her rhythms of the sheep and cows that have come:
we learn to separate and stable them by sex,
let the births happen in the spring with plenty;
soon we build the fire high with rowan branches
as the grain cakes are made with rosemary.
After they bake, we wipe the ash on the cattle's heads, the sheep's
    wool
to protect them for the summer pasturing,
walking them in rings around the cracking fire,
the sheep jumping the coals later as the stars shine like chips of ice
    overhead.

Burn the wood, scatter the coals
fur and skin, fire within
let protection begin:
living meadow, fire a god
ash the holy cushion spoken by stars.

We claim connections, doors, windows and pockets,
we tie and strengthen the cords living between the moon and our
    bodies,
between the animals and their thrumming
swaying, slotting into the spaces of our bodies
where they fit, seamlessly: joined twinnings.

Long Meg and Her Daughters:
A Final Cup and Rings

Speak Thou, whose massy strength and stature scorn
The power of years—pre-eminent, and placed
Apart, to overlook the circle vast.
Speak, Giant-mother!
—William Wordsworth, "The Monument Commonly Called Long Meg and Her Daughters," 1833

i.

The largest stone now carved:
three concentric circles of sun and moon,
cup and ring like mother and child,
death in the fire and flood,
constant winter and spring.
Birth of another mirror for the sky.

Chips of her we place into small woven pouches;
we find a tree with a wound, fingers prying its tacky blood,
push the shards of stone into the resin and shape
small moons: waning, waxing, full. New, rubbed with ash,
darker than the others. All placed back into the pouches
and we carry her with us through generations.

In other lifetimes she will become a coarse, petrified giantess,
a woman who profaned the preferred religion at the time,
branded a witch, her whole coven cast into stone.
A fossilized wedding party given to sin.

ii.

Are the stones the same number? Count them clockwise
and widdershins—they began as seventy-seven but time
has buried some, felled others, and the two cairn alters
that stood in the circle have long crumbled. Count them,
but be careful. Are there fifty-nine backward and
forward? If the number is wrong you could be reduced to a pebble,
carried in a woven pouch because the time for chipping has passed;
harm the tall, thin woman and you unleash harsh storms, poor
harvests and she will bleed, same as any living creature.
You will bleed with her.

Swinside: Holy Engineering

We listen, learn relationship,
study the patterns of fish scales, flower petals
of the stars above and the rocks under our feet.
Touch the spirals of a pinecone, a snail's shell, a ram's horn.
See. The never-ending patterns of leaves, tree branches and limbs.
Closer, now—an apple's core, beeswax cells:
measurement, solid and sure.

We bounce off these patterns,
molding, rotting, blossoming and changing;
sharing stories: vessels of particles,
bumptious, desirous of connection and understanding
as we align ourselves with the stars' patterns,
those sublime circles. We listen as the light's steady telling
shows the measurements and so
we mark the earth, dig and secure stones where lichens will grow,
where cracks form, where ancient memories are embedded,
mark where they will comfortably live in the soil;
come to know us through our songs and breath,
give them a new home in this circle.

Time, that cyclical ancestor, is like a
snake's skin, is a slow-motion
deep dance affording the stones' wiser agency;
we learn to see with these first eyes of the world
in dialogue with the sky
as we continue to lay this circle, this unity, potential.

We make this seed, move its shape 60 times,
carve these rough stones that scuff and callous themselves in our heart,
bring ourselves closer to sky's energy.
This magic is embodied in our bones as we become
a key, turning in a lock,
laid in this circle: knitted intimacy.

Loch an Duin Crannog, Scotland

We peregrinate for days to reach the island;
while henge ditches contain water, sanctifying
cup and ring, rain doesn't hold the same power
as the loch. Our hearts uncertain and humble,
we carry our drinking bowls, dirt and sweat
staining them, readying them
for scrying the sweet, salvific waters.

After we settle, the food is prepared, eaten,
the mead emptied from our bowls, replaced
with river's surface, our fingerprints, stars and moon
shining up from between our hands.

Now is the moment our voices open,
bless our bodies, use our eyes and minds to see
into the wisdom of tomorrows
dancing between the water and moon.

Later, as our eyes stare overhead
slipping with sleep, the stars' plow
promises a fertile harvest.

Some of us offer the loch the hours of
hands shaping clay, meditative mark making,
fire's work of heat and hardening,
letting the bowls slip away in the stream.

Crickets and corncrakes lullaby us through the night.

Brynn Celli Ddu: Mound in the Dark Grove

Come gather to sing the songs of stone,
the songs of rose and apple, heady and ripe
as we place the stag's horn at the henge door with
his skull, the seat of his voice, his eyes, his mind:
we wed him to this world again
we tether him to the divine—
he is man, husband, father, deer.

He is free now to roam the woods
free to mate with the goddess
free to be born anew among the stones
under the stones, within the womb of bank and ditch,
within the secrets the stones keep,
the sun's light shining full on summer morn.

These horns, his crown, will burn with his body:
bones with bones.

We light the wood
like his vitality.
We move around the stones
so he is everlasting.
We gift him back to this earth,
let his spirit fly into the cool, divine light:
cauldron of stars.

Over the days as his bones burn
we stir them, let them cool,
collect them in this clay pot to be planted in the womb,
this tumulus. He is a stag of the sacred wood
returning to feed the world again.

When his power is needed
we will collect it on a summer's day,
after he's been bathed in light,
place his ashes at the center alter,
darken our cheeks with him, flower crowns adorning our heads,
moving to this rhythm of landscape.

Meini Hirion, Wales: Lunating

It is an evening for the children to learn the ways in which they are
the moon,
sitting atop the ring and ditch to watch this calendar rise to replace
the dying sun.

Each child has picked nettle, violet, madder and meadow sweet
to make incense: they squeeze and wrap the bundles
with cordage, begin the singing:
The moon shapes us a cauldron of change,
snake woman shedding her skin:
hole in the stone, let us be reborn.
The others follow in turn.

Mothers, fathers, aunts and uncles with their mortars and pestles
match the song's rhythm as they grind dried berries and herbs,
sprinkle the oil and prepare anointings.

When the incense is bundled, bound with song many times over,
they will hang them to dry until the moon shows her full face
again.
They will learn to read the moon's language,
embrace change and movement,
mimicking the way a woman's belly swells,
the ways field and woods grow full and heavy
yielding the fruits of life and light.
They will learn to become flexible, adapt: they will learn to lunate.

As their eyes grow full of the fire's smoke and night's length,
small hands carry their serpent stones to be anointed
by their families, so those who carry them may remain healthy.

It is said if one desires, they can look through the hole
and the possibilities of the future
are revealed;
we are infinite.

Ballynoe, Ireland: Turning Seasons

With spring's arrival comes lamb and milk,
rich as the woman of green and shoots, sacred springs;
the old ditch around its fountain is the light of stars,
her murmuring cellar and you sing her awakening.
You remember where the red goosefoot, speedwell
and gorse grow to gather and make medicines;
the moon is a spore of the stars—that seed is planted in you;
grow and wax, bring seeds to the fire to bless them
in its smoke—benediction of the sun, heat and holding
to be shaken down into soil.

Heartbeats and tide
back in the blood
seed sower, brother and lover
womb of possibility.

Beginnings of summer: a second turn.
You harvest the elderflower to ferment,
braid crowns of clover, yarrow, dandelion and sage
bathing your face in the dew as you begin to walk the circle,
cradling shells filled with water,
insects buzzing and biting your head
as the sun grows warmer each day
to feed the fields, the woods, all.

Feral beauty
in the mouth of all who speak
in the heart of us who reach
to the stars and earth.

We stand together
breathe the fiery sun
drink the water,
blood of the world.

When the sun sets herds jump the fire
acquiescing to its blessings so they can move to
fertile meadows that make more milk for their young:
grow the herd, secure the tribe, rekindle plants' growth.
You pray for fat bellies and thick heat before the last turn: harvest.

You enter the circle, arms heavy with baskets of shined barley,
fresh fruit and greens, cows and sheep, stocky for slaughter.
The children lay flower garlands on the inner ring of stones:
pinks, whites and yellows among the many greens of leaves and
stalks.
The higher, outer stones laid by the elders are more secure,
intricately patterned after many harvests' worth of practice.

You listen to the haw, tip its waxy berries into the pots
to grind and cook later; sweet drink during winter.
You strip the shepherd's purse to dry for food when the meadows
are covered with white, move your body with thanks for
wild garlic, cabbage, potatoes boiled in a pot, barley and butter
thick and hot,
fruits mashed with the herd's sweet cream, frothy and light.

Sheaves cut, boughs shake, sheep bleat.
Bread baked; food stored.
Dance among the braken and hart's tongue:
the circle ever-moving.

Summer dies and you embrace
the wisdom of those who have passed the veil:
bonfires of oak thanking the harvest's length and blessings,
singing the sheep and cow to bed
dressed in their hides, antlers on your head,
vines in your hair, the smoke and light clearing the way
for the songs of the past wheel turns,
drumming echoing off the trees,
leaves strung yellow, brown and red
at your feet.

Cauldron of change
ring around the stone
as above, so below
beauty of the sleeping land
between dark and light, you stand.

Avebury Henge: What Trees Remember

As a general truth, landscapes change slowly
but our woodland
disappeared in a calculated frenzy:
stone axes and fires.
The noise and movement heralded disaster:
as we burned and fell,
were wrenched away from the soil,
splintered wood and soot,
disturbed birds and bats darkened the sky,
insects buzzed past falling leaves and limbs,
mice, badgers, fox and vole darted directionless
to escape vibrations, smoke, debris.

And so each year nested into the others.
We remaining oaks, alders, and high elms
witnessed other changes as tall, limbless posts
were sunk deep into soil, outlining
where the two-legs were to dig,
deep and round, a moor on the hill,
a ditch enclosed by banks of chalk and grass.

Our deep roots were torn from the earth,
mycelium networks irrevocably damaged,
soil stripped and small rocks moved to mounds,
meters high, around the outside of the posts
as a henge was made: a wave without water.
From above it looked to be a snake eating itself,
a pregnant belly, a fist, the center of a flower, a seed.

Woodhenge, Salisbury, England: What Holds a Culture Together

We begin with stone axes and song to fell the trees, strip the bark
spades of cow's shoulders in hand,
bodies bent over, where the poles will stand staring at sky's face,
digging. Like break water eroding the shoreline, we erode these woods.

We build by the ocean, our younger ones
weaving and knotting nets for fishing
once the trees and dirt tire their bodies.
We work in rhythm with the tides,
the tides in rhythm with the moon,
the moon a rhythm for our bodies.

The trees felled and stars above:
grains of salt mirroring one another.
Timbers below, stars overhead,
moving ever away from each other;
a book read and reread,
written holy like fists or eyes, our belly's buttons,
a flower's center.

And over many lifetimes,
when our ancestors remove the posts
to build stronger, with stone,
they leave the strips of cloth tied with numinous prayers and
    offerings
for rich harvests, plentiful babies, reciprocal love, an easy death
to the surrounding trees,
and fill the holes with chalk,
white as the moon.

Calanais Standing Stones, Scotland: Failure: A Call and Response to the World

Awareness dwells
in the spaces between the stones and sky,
the pockets that intersect within and between
your body, a bee sipping nectar,
a child laying with even breath,
a sheep chewing grass.

The present volleys between all, guides you
to another as you stare into each other's eyes
illuminated by the fire's light
bringing forth the words, singing
as she stands in the center, altar
before her, tribes surrounding her.

Your doubt is buoyed with experience:
fledglings falling from nests, worm into moth;
we're vulnerable between stories,
our past holds songs no one remembers how to sing.

You ask these Callanish stones
to hold your stumblings,
wed your wounds to the earth as
pine branches anointed with ocean's salted water
kiss your shoulders and head,
breach your body bared under the moon's waxing
your heart curled like snail's shell, spiral of movement,
pinprick of light.

Push them down, meld them,
transform them to forward movement,
lessons gained:
all that falls will rise again.

Fach Goch, Wales: A Menhir

Take her in—a little over two meters tall,
five generations of bones buried near her base.

What rituals ceased to rub upon
the hairs on our skin? What unspoken
agreements shrunk into nothingness;
a dried leaf withering on a vine?

We can never know if she was part of a henge
with lost sisters or was erected alone, last of her kind;
a single long stone, premonition of separation,
individuation that has come to pass:

stark reminder that dances of interdependence
are no longer a covenant that surrounds her,
loss of knowing we are part of symbiotic networks
of mycelium, soil, air, land;

foreshadower of stories existing without breath,
reminder of growing disconnect:
today's bodies are filled with chemicals,
placed in cement, no longer able to give back to the land,
feed the earth.

How lonely; we all long for the source
even after death.

She is beginnings of the ardent sowing of land
morphed into ownership
and boundaries
and separateness;
a single marker for graves and grief.

Or she could be a pathway, portal back to
older ways of existing and interacting; a sign
to reintegrate ourselves to the soil—to give back
not only in death,
but in life as well.

We could listen again to the plants,
relearn their lessons of trust, diversity,
co-existence, could help each other flourish
where we are planted, could choose to embrace
the sorrow of what was so we can move into the source
once again, not so lonely and adrift.

The inquiry of what we can recover
is an important path to walk down.

Could our story come full circle
like a henge, like a
cup and its ring?

About the Author

Loralee Clark is a poet and artist who grew up learning a love for nature and her place in it, in Maine. Her first chapbook, *Solemnity Rites* (Prolific Pulse Press, 2025), is an account of reimagined myths and truths of who we are as humans and how we live our histories. Her second chapbook, *Delighting in "To Be": Poems for Writers* (Bottlecap Press, 2025), is a celebration and introspection of the process of writing. Her third, *A Harmony in the Key of Trees: A Healing Myth* (Dancing Girl Press, 2025), examines how a child grows up unconsciously looking to her ecosystem to parent and nurture her. She resides in Virginia and was nominated for three 2026 Pushcart Prizes.

Website:
sites.google.com/view/loraleeclark

Substack:
nosuchthingasfailure.substack.com

www.ingramcontent.com/pod-product-compliance
Lightning Source LLC
LaVergne TN
LVHW090538110826
845146LV00003B/1164

9798901468241